A GIFT FOR:

FROM:

Published by Hallmark Gift Books,
a division of Hallmark Cards, Inc.,
Kansas City, MO 64141
Visit us on the Web at Hallmark.com.

Editorial Director: Delia Berrigan
Editor: Kim Schworm Acosta
Art Director: Chris Opheim
Designer: Brian Pilachowski
Production Designer: Dan Horton

ISBN: 978-1-59530-800-9
BOK2233

Made in China
AUG15

LIFE REFLECTIONS

SHORE
LINES

FROM THE BEACH

Hallmark

CLOUDS
-MAY-
HIDE THE SUN
BUT ONLY FOR
A LITTLE WHILE.

EVERY DAY

&

EVERY TIDE

bring new treasures
to your shores.

Being
true to
yourself
comes with
scary moments.

But it's so very worth it.

Make time to PLAY.

EVEN THE SUN NEEDS DOWNTIME.

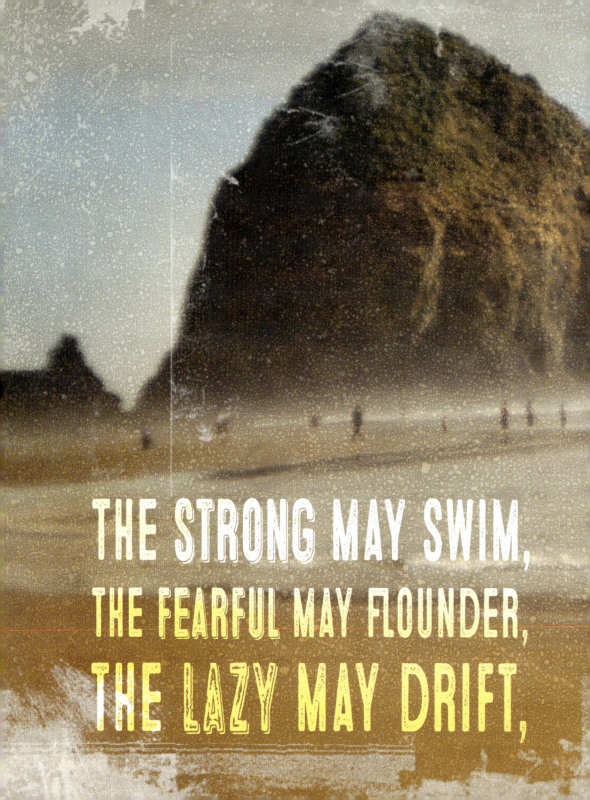

THE STRONG MAY SWIM,
THE FEARFUL MAY FLOUNDER,
THE LAZY MAY DRIFT,

BUT THE OCEAN CARRIES THEM ALL.

COLLECT
SMALL
JOYS.

Wherever you go,
leave a trail of
HAPPY

MEMORIES.

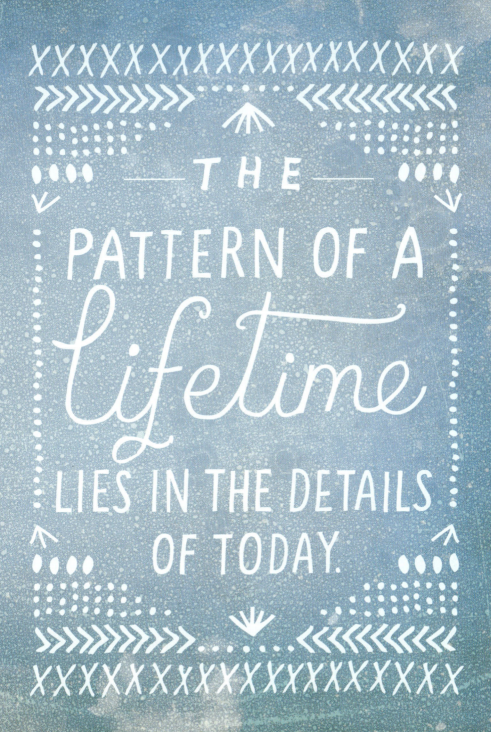

THE
PATTERN OF A
lifetime
LIES IN THE DETAILS
OF TODAY.

Rest upon the cool grass.

Linger in the golden sun.

Dream beneath the bright blue sky.

THE TIDE

ALWAYS TURNS.

Each of us carries a

SUNRISE

within.

THERE IS MEANING
IN SILENCE
AS WELL AS
IN WORDS.

SEEK WHAT
♒ THE SOUL

CRAVES.

Sometimes it helps just to know

YOU'RE NOT ALONE.

Nobody else's

FOOT

STEPS

*lead exactly
where you're going.*

TELL YOUR STORY
& BE THE LIGHT
THAT HELPS OTHERS
FIND THEIR WAY.

LOOK AROUND.
LIFE COMES *with*

a GREAT VIEW.

We marvel at the POWER
Yet, within each

of the sea.
of us is a FORCE
that's mightier.

Life is like a day at the beach—

if you're not careful,
YOU'LL GET BURNED.
If you're too careful,
YOU WON'T HAVE ANY FUN.

We will be known
FOREVER BY

THE RIPPLES
we create.

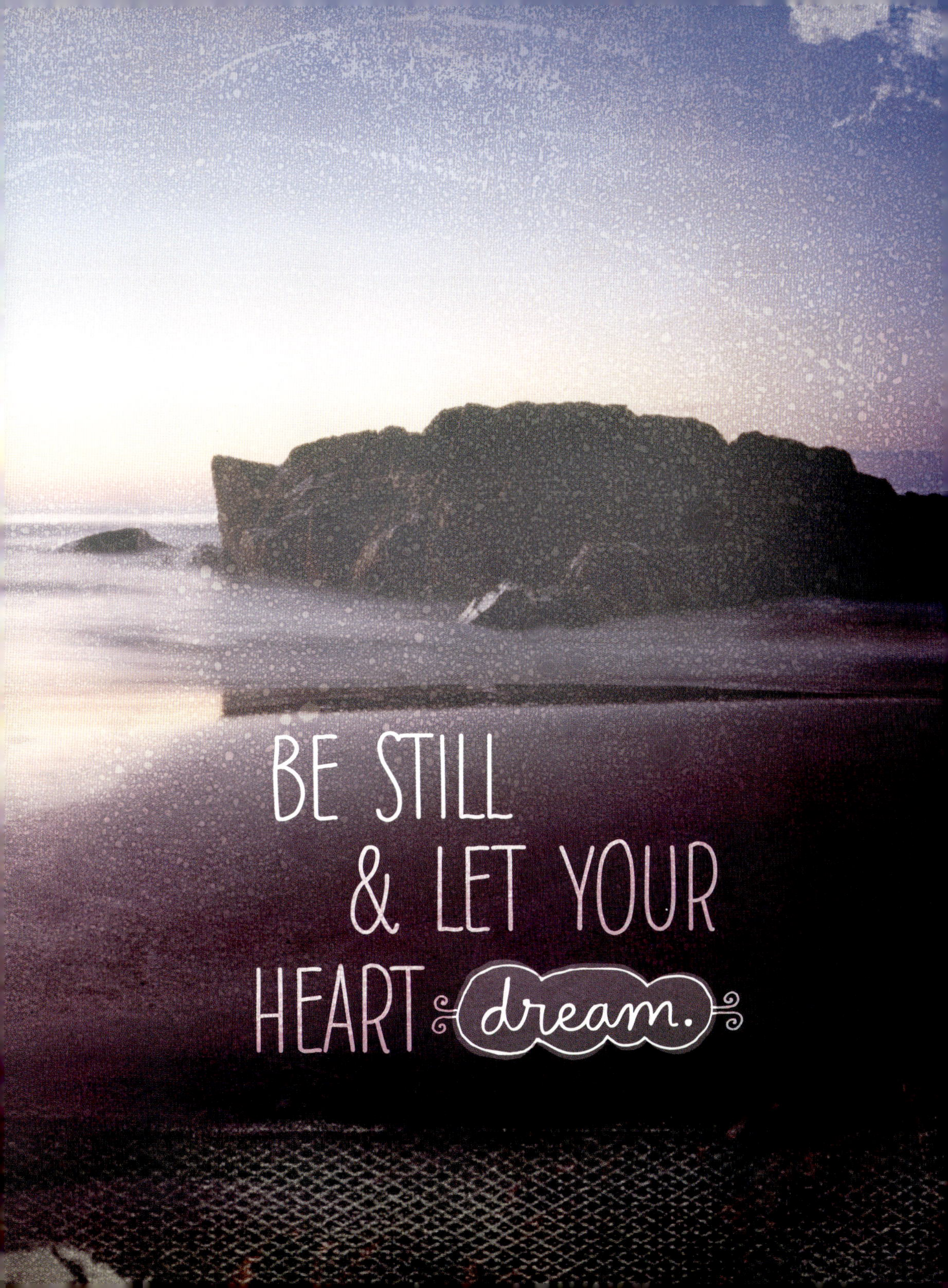
BE STILL
& LET YOUR
HEART dream.

For every
—JOY—
that passes,
something
❧ BEAUTIFUL ❧
remains.

GO IN THE DIRECTION
THAT BECKONS TO YOU ...

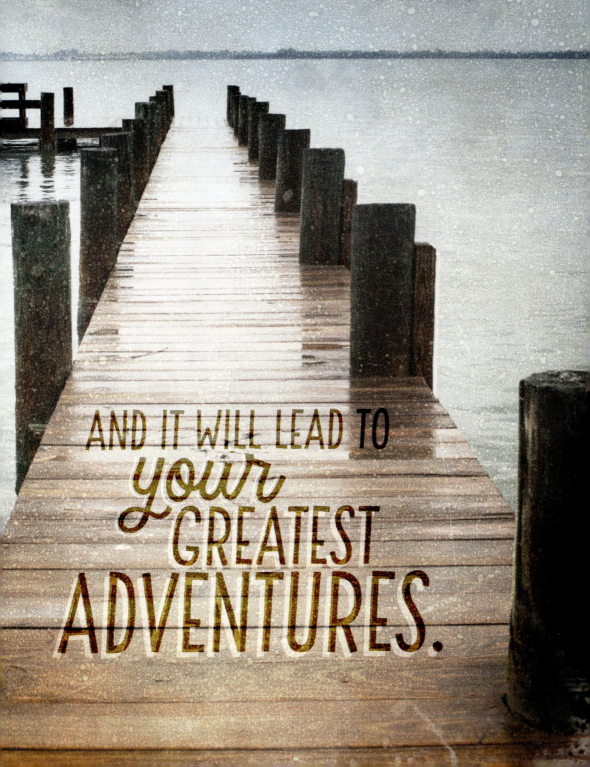

WAVES

MAKE

WAVES

MAKE

WAVES.

DO your THING.

=A NEW=

DREAM

IS ALWAYS, ALWAYS

SHIMMERING

=ON THE=

HORIZON.

when the
TIDE IS LOW.

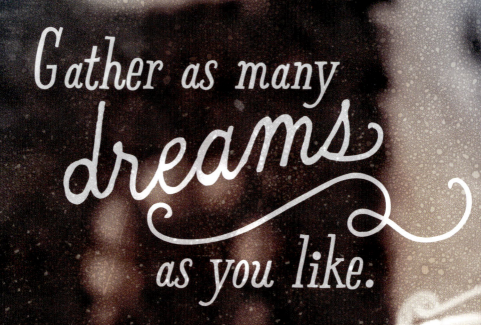

Gather as many *dreams* as you like.

No one needs to

Toss worries to the *breeze*.

BEAUTY AROUND US,

Like the smell of SALT
in your hair,
like warm SAND
between your toes,
let HAPPINESS stay
with you all day long.

If you have enjoyed this book
or it has touched your life in some way,
we would love to hear from you.

Please send your comments to:
Hallmark Book Feedback
P.O. Box 419034
Mail Drop 100
Kansas City, MO 64141

Or e-mail us at:
booknotes@hallmark.com